Charlotte Zolotow

Some Things Go Together

PICTURES BY

Karen Gundersheimer

A Harper Trophy Book
Harper & Row, Publishers

Some Things Go Together
Text copyright © 1969 by Charlotte Zolotow
Illustrations copyright © 1983 by Karen Gundersheimer
All rights reserved. No part of this book may be
used or reproduced in any manner whatsoever without
written permission except in the case of brief quotations
embodied in critical articles and reviews. Printed in
the United States of America. For information address
Harper & Row Junior Books, 10 East 53rd Street,
New York, N.Y. 10022. Published simultaneously in
Canada by Fitzhenry & Whiteside Limited, Toronto.
First Harper Trophy edition, 1987.
Published in hardcover by Thomas Y. Crowell, New York.

Library of Congress Cataloging in Publication Data
Zolotow, Charlotte, 1915–
    Some things go together.

    Summary: Illustrations accompany couplets
describing things that go together naturally, such
as "Sand with sea" and especially "you with me."
    1. Children's poetry, American.   [1. American
poetry] I. Gundersheimer, Karen ill.   II. Title.
PS3549.0636S6   1983   811'.54   82-48694
ISBN 0-690-04327-9
ISBN 0-690-04328-7 (lib. bdg.)

    (A Harper Trophy book)
ISBN 0-06-443133-9 (pbk.)

Peace with dove
Home with love

Gardens with flowers

Clocks with hours

Moths with screen

Grass with green

Leaves with tree
and you with me

Witch with broom
Bowl with spoon

Mountains with high

Birds with fly

Pigeons with park

Stars with dark

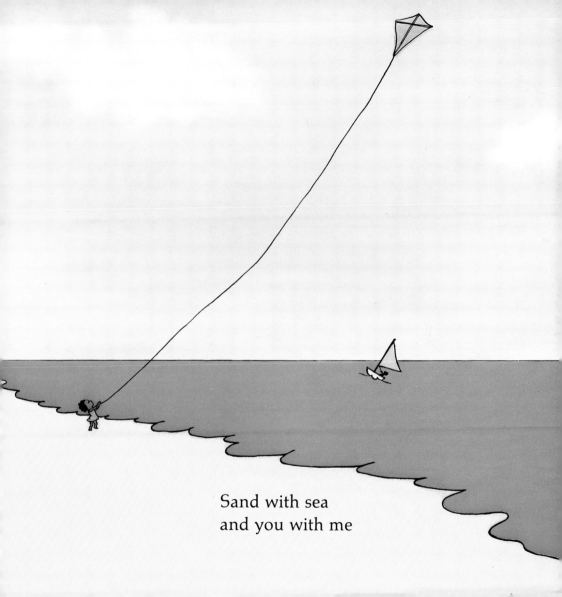

Sand with sea
and you with me

Music with dance

Horses with prance

Hats with heads

Pillows with beds

Franks with beans

Kings with queens

Lions with zoo
and me with you

White with snow
Wind with blow

Moon with night

Sun with light

Sky with blue
AND ME WITH YOU!